Level One: Book 1
Breakthrough to Math

Understanding Numbers

Materials were developed by the Glassboro State College Adult Education Resource Center in cooperation with New Jersey State Department of Education, Division of School Programs, Bureau of Adult Continuing Education.

Materials do not necessarily reflect NJ State Department of Education Policy and no official endorsement should be inferred.

Edited by Ann K.U. Tussing

Curriculum developers: Barbara Banks
Loretta Pullano

New Readers Press • Box 131 • Syracuse, New York 13210

Table of Contents

Pre-test 3

Introduction 5

  1. Counting 6

  2. Numerals and number words 13

  3. 1-place numbers 18

  4. 2-place numbers 21

  5. More 2-place numbers 26

  6. Values of 2-place numbers 33

  7. Finding values of 2-place numbers
      when the tens are the same 37

  8. 3-place numbers 41

  9. 4-place numbers 45

10. Place values in 1- to 7-place numbers 49

11. Money numbers 53

12. Writing checks 57

Post-test 63

Designed by Caris Lester,
Marsha Shur, and Chris Doolittle
Typeset by Chris Doolittle
Cover by Caris Lester

ISBN 0-88336-810-2

© 1978 Glassboro State College, Glassboro, New Jersey.
  Revised 1981.

Printed in the United States of America

9 8 7 6 5 4 3

1. How many dots are in the box?

   | • • • • • • |

   _____

2. Write the numeral for this number: **eight** _____

3. Write the word for this number: **3** _____

4. Write the numbers that are left out: **1, 2, _____, 4, 5, _____, 7, _____, 9**

5. How many tens are in the number 32?   _____ **tens**

   How many ones are in the number 32?   _____ **ones**

6. Write the numeral for this number: **sixty** _____

7. Write the word for this number: **74** _____

8. Which number is biggest? Circle it.   **26   35   62**

9. Which number is biggest? Circle it.   **32   33   31**

10. Write the numeral for this number: **seven hundred eighty-two**_____

11. How many hundreds are in 395?   _____ **hundreds**

12. Write the numeral for this word: **four thousand, five hundred forty-one**

    _____

13. What number comes next?   **9,997   9,998   9,999** _____

14. Write the numeral for this word: **Six thousand, forty-six dollars and two cents**

    _____

15. Write the numeral two ways: **Seventy-two cents**_____

    _____

Answers for pre-test

1. 6
2. 8
3. three
4. 3, 6, 8
5. 3 tens
   2 ones
6. 60
7. seventy-four
8. 62
9. 33
10. 782
11. 3 hundreds
12. 4,541
13. 10,000
14. $6,046.02
15. $.72
    72¢

If you missed this question:	Study these pages:
1 ——————▶	pages 6-12
2 or 3 ——————▶	pages 13-17
4 ——————▶	pages 18-20
5, 6, or 7 ——————▶	pages 21-32
8 ——————▶	pages 33-36
9 ——————▶	pages 37-40
10 or 11 ——————▶	pages 41-44
12 ——————▶	pages 45-48
13 ——————▶	pages 49-52
14 or 15 ——————▶	pages 53-56

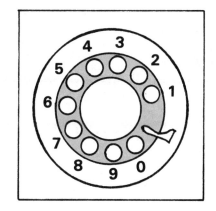

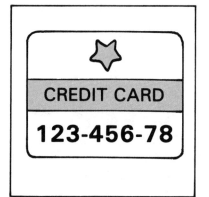

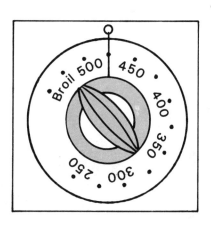

We see numbers every day.
We use numbers every day.

1. Counting

When we count, we say the numbers in order.
Learn to say these numbers:

0

1

2

3

4

5

6

7

8

9

Numerals are the figures we use to write the numbers.
Practice making these numerals:

0 _____

1 _____

2 _____

3 _____

4 _____

5 _____

6 _____

7 _____

8 _____

9 _____

Practice counting

There is nothing in the box.
There are **0** things in the box.

There is **1** dish in the box.

There are **2** pans in the box.
Count them: 1, 2.

There are **3** birds in the box.
Count them: 1, 2, 3.

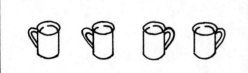

There are **4** cups in the box.
Count them: 1, 2, 3, 4.

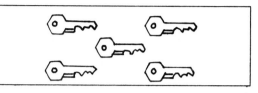

There are **5** keys in the box.
Count them: 1, 2, 3, 4, 5.

There are **6** fish in the box.
Count them: 1, 2, 3, 4, 5, 6.

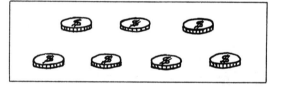

There are **7** quarters in the box.
Count them: 1, 2, 3, 4, 5, 6, 7.

There are **8** apples in the box.
Count them: 1, 2, 3, 4, 5, 6, 7, 8.

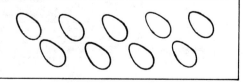

There are **9** eggs in the box.
Count them: 1, 2, 3, 4, 5, 6, 7, 8, 9.

Exercise 1-A

Count the number of stars in each box.
Then draw a line to the correct numeral.
The first line has been drawn for you.

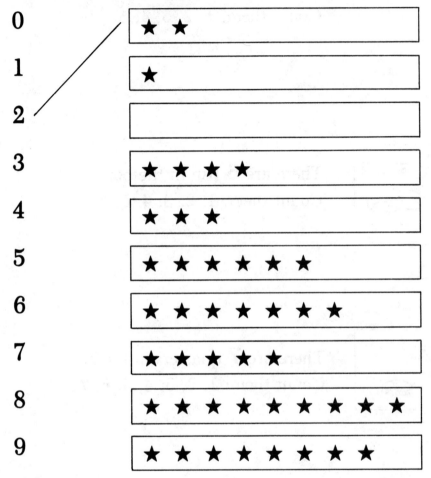

0
1
2
3
4
5
6
7
8
9

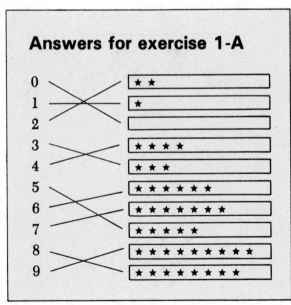

Answers for exercise 1-A

Exercise 1-B

Count the number of things in each box.
Write the numeral next to the box.

Numeral

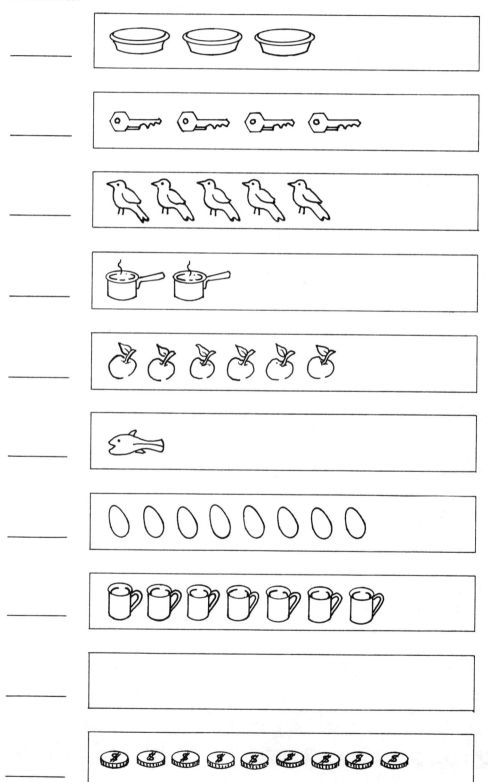

Answers for exercise 1-B are on page 12.

Answers for exercise 1-B

Numeral

_3_

_4_

_5_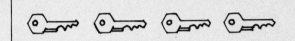

_2_

_6_

_1_

_8_

_7_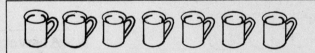

_0_

_9_

2. Numerals and number words

Every number can be written two ways.
It can be written as a numeral.
Or it can be written as a word.
The numeral and word stand for the same thing.

Numeral	Word
0	zero
1	one
2	two
3	three
4	four
5	five
6	six
7	seven
8	eight
9	nine

Practice writing number words

Copy these words for the numbers you have learned.

zero _____

one   _____

two   _____

three _____

four _____

five _____

six   _____

seven _____

eight _____

nine _____

Exercise 2-A

Draw a line from the numeral to the word.
The first line has been drawn for you.

Numeral	Word
0	two
1	zero
2	one
3	four
4	three
5	six
6	seven
7	five
8	nine
9	eight

Answers for exercise 2-A are on page 16.

Exercise 2-B

Look at the numerals below.
Next to each numeral write the *word* for that number.

Numeral	Word
0	_____
1	_____
2	_____
3	_____
4	_____
5	_____
6	_____
7	_____
8	_____
9	_____

Answers for exercise 2-B are on page 16.

Answers for exercise 2-A

Numeral		Word
0		two
1		zero
2		one
3		four
4		three
5		six
6		seven
7		five
8		nine
9		eight

(0→one, 1→two, 2→zero, 3→three, 4→four, 5→five, 6→seven, 7→six, 8→eight, 9→nine)

Answers for exercise 2-B

Numeral	Word
0	zero
1	one
2	two
3	three
4	four
5	five
6	six
7	seven
8	eight
9	nine

Exercise 2-C

Count the number of things in each box.
Write the numeral and word under the box.

Numeral __5__

Word __five__

Numeral _____

Word _____

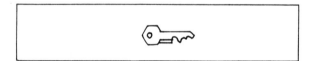

Numeral _____

Word _____

Numeral _____

Word _____

Numeral _____

Word _____

Numeral _____

Word _____

Answers for exercise 2-C	
5	0
five	zero
3	2
three	two
1	
one	
7	
seven	

3. 1-place numbers

All of the numbers from 0 to 9 are called "ones."
They are 1-place numbers.
Each of these numbers tells how many *ones* the number stands for.
The number 2 stands for *two ones*.
The number 4 stands for *four ones*.

Here is a chart that shows all the numbers we have looked at so far.
Next to each number is a box.
It shows how many ones that number stands for.

(The sign = is an *equals* sign.
It means *is the same as*.)

0 = ☐ = 0 ones

1 = [•] = 1 one

2 = [• •] = 2 ones

3 = [• • •] = 3 ones

4 = [• • • •] = 4 ones

5 = [• • • • •] = 5 ones

6 = [• • • • • •] = 6 ones

7 = [• • • • • • •] = 7 ones

8 = [• • • • • • • •] = 8 ones

9 = [• • • • • • • • •] = 9 ones

Some numbers stand for more ones than other numbers.
The number 1 stands for one more than 0.
The number 2 stands for one more than 1.
The number 3 stands for one more than 2.

When a number stands for more ones than another number stands for,
it has more *value*.
Sometimes people say it is *bigger* or *larger*.

Practice with 1-place numbers

All of the numbers we have worked with so far are shown below.
The numbers are in order of their value.
They start with the smallest value, 0.
They end with the largest value, 9.

This is the number order we use when we count.
We call this line a *number line*.

Exercise 3

Below are some number lines.
Fill in the missing numbers on each line.

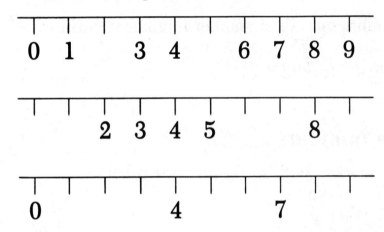

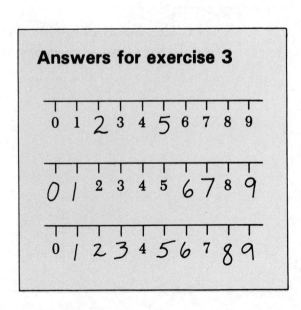

Answers for exercise 3

4. 2-place numbers

The numbers from 0 to 9 are called 1-place numbers.
They are written with one numeral.

Each number in order from 0 to 9 is one more than
the previous number.
The number 1 is one more than 0.
The number 2 is one more than 1.
The number 9 is one more than 8.

What number is one more than 9?
The number 10 (ten) is one more than 9.

10

The number 10 is a 2-place number.
It is written with two numerals, 1 and 0.

Here is a number line.
It shows that 2-place numbers come after 1-place numbers.
You can see that 10 is one more than 9.

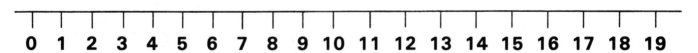

0 1 2 3 4 5 6 7 8 9 10 11 12 13 14 15 16 17 18 19

Practice with 2-place numbers

Learn to say these 2-place numbers:

Numeral	Word
10	ten
11	eleven
12	twelve
13	thirteen
14	fourteen
15	fifteen
16	sixteen
17	seventeen
18	eighteen
19	nineteen

Now write the numerals and words you just learned.

Numeral	Word
_____	_____
_____	_____
_____	_____
_____	_____
_____	_____
_____	_____
_____	_____
_____	_____
_____	_____
_____	_____

Every 2-place number tells how many tens and ones the number stands for.

The number 10 stands for 1 ten and 0 ones.

The number 11 stands for 1 ten and 1 one.

Look at the numbers from 10 to 19.

Numeral		Tens	Ones
10	=	1	0
11	=	1	1
12	=	1	2
13	=	1	3
14	=	1	4
15	=	1	5
16	=	1	6
17	=	1	7
18	=	1	8
19	=	1	9

Exercise 4

Look at the dot pictures.
Circle the first 10 dots.

How many tens are there? Write that number under *Tens*.
How many ones are there? Write that number under *Ones*.

Then write the numeral for the number of all the dots.
The first dot picture has been done for you.

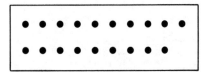

Tens	Ones		Numeral
1	3	=	13

Tens	Ones		Numeral
___	___	=	___

Tens	Ones		Numeral
___	___	=	___

Tens	Ones		Numeral
___	___	=	___

Tens	Ones		Numeral
___	___	=	___

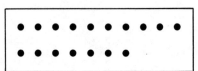

Tens	Ones		Numeral
___	___	=	___

Answers for exercise 4

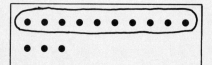

Tens	Ones		Numeral
1	3	=	13

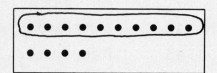

Tens	Ones		Numeral
1	4	=	14

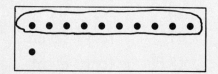

Tens	Ones		Numeral
1	1	=	11

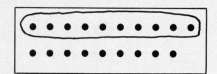

Tens	Ones		Numeral
1	9	=	19

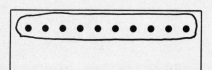

Tens	Ones		Numeral
1	0	=	10

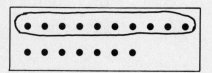

Tens	Ones		Numeral
1	7	=	17

5. More 2-place numbers

The 2-place numbers go from 10 (ten) to 99 (ninety-nine).
We have just learned about the 2-place numbers from 10 to 19.
Now learn the rest of the 2-place numbers:

Numeral	Word	Numeral	Word
20	twenty	40	forty
21	twenty-one	41	forty-one
22	twenty-two	42	forty-two
23	twenty-three	43	forty-three
24	twenty-four	44	forty-four
25	twenty-five	45	forty-five
26	twenty-six	46	forty-six
27	twenty-seven	47	forty-seven
28	twenty-eight	48	forty-eight
29	twenty-nine	49	forty-nine
30	thirty	50	fifty
31	thirty-one	51	fifty-one
32	thirty-two	52	fifty-two
33	thirty-three	53	fifty-three
34	thirty-four	54	fifty-four
35	thirty-five	55	fifty-five
36	thirty-six	56	fifty-six
37	thirty-seven	57	fifty-seven
38	thirty-eight	58	fifty-eight
39	thirty-nine	59	fifty-nine

Numeral	Word	Numeral	Word
60	sixty	80	eighty
61	sixty-one	81	eighty-one
62	sixty-two	82	eighty-two
63	sixty-three	83	eighty-three
64	sixty-four	84	eighty-four
65	sixty-five	85	eighty-five
66	sixty-six	86	eighty-six
67	sixty-seven	87	eighty-seven
68	sixty-eight	88	eighty-eight
69	sixty-nine	89	eighty-nine
70	seventy	90	ninety
71	seventy-one	91	ninety-one
72	seventy-two	92	ninety-two
73	seventy-three	93	ninety-three
74	seventy-four	94	ninety-four
75	seventy-five	95	ninety-five
76	seventy-six	96	ninety-six
77	seventy-seven	97	ninety-seven
78	seventy-eight	98	ninety-eight
79	seventy-nine	99	ninety-nine

Exercise 5-A

Look at each number on the left.
How many tens does it stand for? Write that number under *Tens*.
How many ones does it stand for? Write that number under *Ones*.

	Tens	Ones
23 =	2	3
37 =		
89 =		
40 =		
56 =		
65 =		
17 =		
10 =		
99 =		

Answers for exercise 5-A are on page 30.

Exercise 5-B

Look at the words below.
Next to each word write the *numeral* for that number.

Numeral	Word
_____	twenty-nine
_____	twenty-three
_____	thirty-two
_____	forty
_____	fifty-five
_____	sixty-seven
_____	seventy-six
_____	eighty
_____	ninety-four
_____	ninety-nine

Answers for exercise 5-B are on page 30.

Answers for exercise 5-A

		Tens	Ones
23	=	2	3
37	=	3	7
89	=	8	9
40	=	4	0
56	=	5	6
65	=	6	5
17	=	1	7
10	=	1	0
99	=	9	9

Answers for exercise 5-B

Numeral	Word
29	twenty-nine
23	twenty-three
32	thirty-two
40	forty
55	fifty-five
67	sixty-seven
76	seventy-six
80	eighty
94	ninety-four
99	ninety-nine

Exercise 5-C

Look at the numerals below.
Next to each numeral write the *word* for that number.

Numeral   Word

20   _____

30   _____

40   _____

50   _____

60   _____

70   _____

80   _____

90   _____

25   _____

37   _____

44   _____

51   _____

68   _____

72   _____

83   _____

99   _____

Answers for exercise 5-C are on page 32.

Answers for exercise 5-C

Numeral	Word
20	twenty
30	thirty
40	forty
50	fifty
60	sixty
70	seventy
80	eighty
90	ninety
25	twenty-five
37	thirty-seven
44	forty-four
51	fifty-one
68	sixty-eight
72	seventy-two
83	eighty-three
99	ninety-nine

6. Values of 2-place numbers

You know how to find the value of a 1-place number.
The value is how many ones the number stands for.

2-place numbers are bigger than 1-place numbers.

You can find the value of a 2-place number.
The value is how many tens and ones the number stands for.

Which of these numbers has the most value?
That is, which is the biggest?

29
64
35

Look at the numbers in the tens' place.
They are 2, 6, and 3.
You know that 6 stands for more tens than 2 or 3.
So 64 is the biggest number.
That is, 64 has the most value.

Practice finding values of 2-place numbers

Example: Which is the biggest number?
That is, which has the most value?

12

48

57

Look at the numbers in the tens' place.
They are 1, 4, and 5.
You know that 5 stands for more tens than 1 or 4.
It has more value.
So 57 has the most value.
It is the biggest number.

Exercise 6

Circle the biggest number in each box.
The biggest number in the first box has been circled for you.

27
(82)
34

42
72
92

92
86
31

51
26
60

12
21
90

34
28
77

88
20
55

Answers for exercise 6 are on page 36.

Answers for exercise 6

```
┌─────┐
│ 27  │
│(82) │
│ 34  │
└─────┘

┌─────┐
│ 42  │
│ 72  │
│(92) │
└─────┘

┌─────┐
│(92) │
│ 86  │
│ 31  │
└─────┘

┌─────┐
│ 51  │
│ 26  │
│(60) │
└─────┘

┌─────┐
│ 12  │
│ 21  │
│(90) │
└─────┘

┌─────┐
│ 34  │
│ 28  │
│(77) │
└─────┘

┌─────┐
│(88) │
│ 20  │
│ 55  │
└─────┘
```

7. Finding values of 2-place numbers when the tens are the same

Which is the biggest number?
That is, which has the most value?

21

29

27

Look at the numbers in the tens' place.
They are all 2s!
So we have to look at the ones' place to find which number is biggest.

The numbers in the ones' place are 1, 9, and 7.
We know that 9 stands for more ones than 1 or 7.
So 29 is the biggest number.
That is, 29 has the most value.

Practice finding values of 2-place numbers when the tens are the same

Example: Which is the biggest number?
That is, which has the most value?

33

30

37

Look at the numbers in the tens' place.
They are all 3s!
So look at the numbers in the ones' place.
They are 3, 0, and 7.
We know that 7 stands for more ones than 0 or 3.
So 37 is the biggest number.
It has the most value.

Exercise 7

Circle the biggest number in each box.

| 14 |
| 17 |
| 18 |

| 50 |
| 52 |
| 53 |

| 63 |
| 67 |
| 61 |

| 46 |
| 43 |
| 41 |

| 17 |
| 16 |
| 14 |

| 88 |
| 87 |
| 86 |

| 73 |
| 76 |
| 75 |

Answers for exercise 7 are on page 40.

Finding values of 2-place numbers
when the tens are the same / **39**

Answers for exercise 7

14
17
(18)

50
52
(53)

63
(67)
61

(46)
43
41

(17)
16
14

(88)
87
86

73
(76)
75

8. 3-place numbers

The number 99 is the biggest 2-place number.
The next number in order is 100 (one hundred).

100 is one more than 99.
It is a 3-place number.
It has three numerals: 1, 0, and 0.
They stand for 1 hundred, 0 tens, and 0 ones.

The biggest 3-place number is 999 (nine hundred ninety-nine).
It stands for 9 hundreds, 9 tens, and 9 ones.

Every 3-place number tells how many hundreds, tens, and ones the number stands for.

Practice writing 3-place numbers

There are many 3-place numbers.
Here are some of them:

Numeral	Word
200	two hundred
201	two hundred one
210	two hundred ten
318	three hundred eighteen
400	four hundred
560	five hundred sixty
821	eight hundred twenty-one
932	nine hundred thirty-two

Copy the numerals and words for these 3-place numbers.

Numeral	Word
____	_____
____	_____
____	_____
____	_____
____	_____
____	_____
____	_____
____	_____

Exercise 8

Write the numeral next to each word.

Numeral	Word
_____	two hundred thirty-six
_____	five hundred forty-eight
_____	seven hundred
_____	nine hundred seventeen
_____	nine hundred ninety-nine

Write the word next to each numeral.

Numeral	Word
194	_____
800	_____
303	_____

Answers for exercise 8 are on page 44.

Answers for exercise 8

Numeral	Word
236	two hundred thirty-six
548	five hundred forty-eight
700	seven hundred
917	nine hundred seventeen
999	nine hundred ninety-nine

Numeral	Word
194	one hundred ninety-four
800	eight hundred
303	three hundred three

9. 4-place numbers

The number 999 is the biggest 3-place number.
The next number in order is 1,000 (one thousand).
It is one more than 999.
It is a 4-place number.
It has four numerals: 1, 0, 0, and 0.
They stand for 1 thousand, 0 hundreds, 0 tens, and 0 ones.

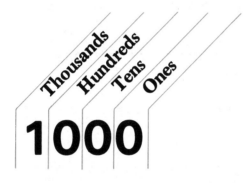

Every 4-place number tells how many thousands, hundreds, tens, and ones the number stands for.

The biggest 4-place number is 9,999
(nine thousand, nine hundred ninety-nine).

9,999

We use a comma after the number in the thousands' place.
The comma makes large numbers easier to read.

Practice with 4-place numbers

There are many 4-place numbers.
Here are some of them:

Numeral	Word
1,295	one thousand, two hundred ninety-five
2,628	two thousand, six hundred twenty-eight
3,453	three thousand, four hundred fifty-three
4,780	four thousand, seven hundred eighty
5,031	five thousand, thirty-one
6,331	six thousand, three hundred thirty-one
7,001	seven thousand, one
8,010	eight thousand, ten
9,817	nine thousand, eight hundred seventeen

Exercise 9

Write the numeral next to each word.

Numeral	Word
_____	two thousand, five hundred forty-six
_____	five thousand, three hundred eighteen
_____	six thousand, one hundred twenty-one
_____	seven thousand, nine hundred three
_____	eight thousand, one

Write the word next to each numeral.

Numeral	Word
1,381	_____
	_____
6,000	_____
	_____
7,122	_____
	_____

Answers for exercise 9 are on page 48.

Answers for exercise 9

Numeral	Word
2,546	two thousand, five hundred forty-six
5,318	five thousand, three hundred eighteen
6,121	six thousand, one hundred twenty-one
7,903	seven thousand, nine hundred three
8,001	eight thousand, one

Numeral	Word
1,381	one thousand, three hundred eighty-one
6,000	six thousand
7,122	seven thousand, one hundred twenty-two

10. Place values in 1- to 7-place numbers

The biggest numeral in any place is 9.

9
10

The biggest 1-place number is 9 (nine).
The number after 9 is 10 (ten).
Ten is a 2-place number.

99
100

The biggest 2-place number is 99 (ninety-nine).
The number after 99 is 100 (one hundred).
One hundred is a 3-place number.

999
1,000

The biggest 3-place number is 999
(nine hundred ninety-nine).
The number after 999 is 1,000 (one thousand).
One thousand is a 4-place number.

9,999
10,000

The biggest 4-place number is 9,999
(nine thousand, nine hundred ninety-nine).
The number after 9,999 is 10,000 (ten thousand).
Ten thousand is a 5-place number.

99,999
100,000

The biggest 5-place number is 99,999 (ninety-nine
thousand, nine hundred ninety-nine).
The number after 99,999 is 100,000
(one hundred thousand).
One hundred thousand is a 6-place number.

999,999
1,000,000

The biggest 6-place number is 999,999 (nine hundred
ninety-nine thousand, nine hundred ninety-nine).
The number after 999,999 is 1,000,000 (one million).
One million is a 7-place number.

Our number system is based on 10.
Every place is worth 10 of the place before.

Millions	Hundred thousands	Ten thousands	Thousands	Hundreds	Tens	Ones	
					1	0	A ten is 10 ones.
				1	0	0	A hundred is 10 tens.
			1,	0	0	0	A thousand is 10 hundreds.
		1	0,	0	0	0	Ten thousand is 10 thousands.
	1	0	0,	0	0	0	A hundred thousand is 10 ten thousands.
1,	0	0	0,	0	0	0	A million is 10 hundred thousands.

Now you can see the pattern of our number system.
The more places there are, the bigger the number.
The number 40 is bigger than 4.
The number 11,000 is bigger than 9,000.
The number 2,000,000 is bigger than 898,998.

Practice with larger numbers

Millions	Hundred thousands	Ten thousands	Thousands	Hundreds	Tens	Ones	Word	Numeral
		6	5,	0	0	0	sixty-five thousand	65,000
		7	3,	8	1	9	seventy-three thousand, eight hundred nineteen	73,819
	6	0	0,	0	0	0	six hundred thousand	600,000
	8	6	0,	7	2	5	eight hundred sixty thousand, seven hundred twenty-five	860,725
6,	0	0	0,	0	0	0	six million	6,000,000
7,	5	0	0,	0	0	0	seven million, five hundred thousand	7,500,000
8,	2	1	9,	8	7	6	eight million, two hundred nineteen thousand, eight hundred seventy-six	8,219,876

Exercise 10

Draw a line from the numeral to the word.

Numeral	Word
60,000	eighty-four thousand
84,000	six thousand
6,000	sixty thousand
5,000,000	six hundred thousand
600,000	six million
10,300	five million
780,321	ten thousand, three hundred
6,000,000	seven hundred eighty thousand, three hundred twenty-one

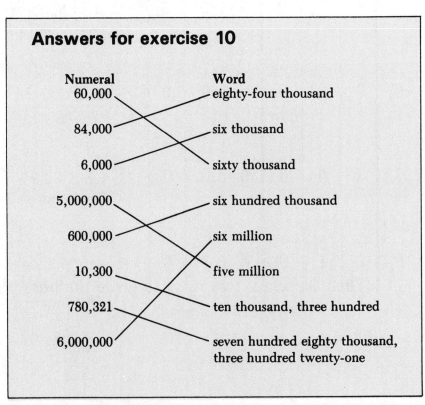

Answers for exercise 10

Numeral	Word
60,000	eighty-four thousand
84,000	six thousand
6,000	sixty thousand
5,000,000	six hundred thousand
600,000	six million
10,300	five million
780,321	ten thousand, three hundred
6,000,000	seven hundred eighty thousand, three hundred twenty-one

11. Money numbers

Money numbers are written in words or numerals.

Word   **Numeral**
Seventeen dollars and $17.85
eighty-five cents

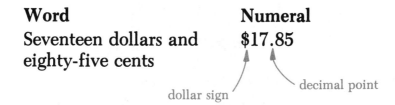

Sometimes you have just dollars and no cents.
Then write two zeros (00) after the decimal point.

Word   **Numeral**
Seventeen dollars $17.00

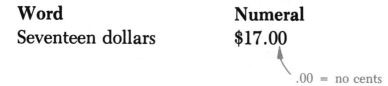

.00 = no cents

Sometimes you have dollars and less than ten cents.
Then use a zero after the decimal point as a place holder.

Word   **Numeral**
Seventeen dollars and $17.06
six cents

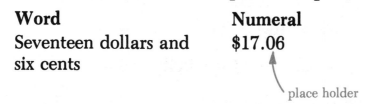

place holder

Sometimes you have just cents and no dollars.
Then there are two ways to write the numeral.

Word   **Numeral**
Twenty cents $.20   or   20¢

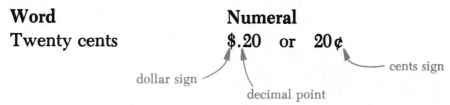

Place value is very important for writing money numbers.
There is a big difference between these numbers:

$.10 (Ten cents)

$1.00 (One dollar)

$10.00 (Ten dollars)

$100.00 (One hundred dollars)

$1,000.00 (One thousand dollars)

You wouldn't want to pay $1.00 for a $.10 stamp!
You wouldn't want your boss to pay you $10.00 when she owes you $100.00!

Practice with money numbers

Numeral	Word
$.07	Seven cents
$.70	Seventy cents
89¢	Eighty-nine cents
$15.53	Fifteen dollars and fifty-three cents
$25.00	Twenty-five dollars
$240.03	Two hundred forty dollars and three cents
$65,750.00	Sixty-five thousand, seven hundred fifty dollars

Exercise 11

Write the numeral for each money number.

Numeral	Word
_____	Two dollars and ninety-five cents
_____	Seventy-five dollars and five cents
_____	One hundred dollars
_____	Sixty cents
_____	Three hundred dollars and fifty cents
_____	Four thousand dollars and ten cents

Write the word for each money number.

Numeral	Word
$3.00	_____
$.10	_____
90¢	_____
$10.25	_____

Answers for exercise 11 are on page 56.

Answers for exercise 11

Numeral	Word
$2.95	Two dollars and ninety-five cents
$75.05	Seventy-five dollars and five cents
$100.00	One hundred dollars
$.60 or 60¢	Sixty cents
$300.50	Three hundred dollars and fifty cents
$4,000.10	Four thousand dollars and ten cents

Numeral	Word
$3.00	Three dollars
$.10	Ten cents
90¢	Ninety cents
$10.25	Ten dollars and twenty-five cents

12. Writing checks

To write a check, we have to write down the amount of money twice.

On one line, we write the total amount in numerals.

On the next line, we write the dollar amount in words.
Then we write the cents amount in numerals over 100.
We do this because there are one hundred cents in each dollar.

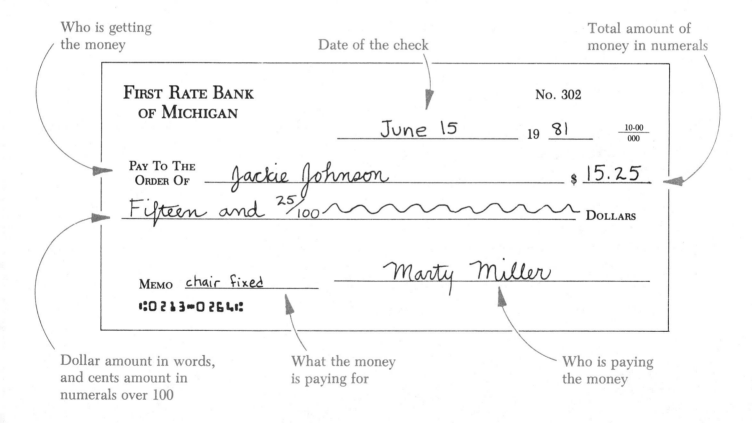

Who is getting the money

Date of the check

Total amount of money in numerals

Dollar amount in words, and cents amount in numerals over 100

What the money is paying for

Who is paying the money

Practice writing checks

Example 1. This check is to Big Value Supermarket from Alan Kelly.
It is for $32.00.

Total amount of
money in numerals

FIRST RATE BANK	No. 427
OF MICHIGAN	

May 17 19 _81_ $\frac{10\text{-}00}{000}$

PAY TO THE
ORDER OF _Big Value Supermarket_ $ _32.00_

Thirty-two and $^{00}/_{100}$ ∿∿∿∿∿∿ DOLLARS

MEMO _groceries + cash_   _Alan Kelly_

⑆0213⬝0264⑆

Dollar amount in words, and cents amount in numerals over 100.
You can write _no cents_ like this: $\frac{00}{100}$ or $\frac{no}{100}$

Example 2.   This check is to Dr. Ruth Miller from Richard Goldstein. It is for $45.00.

FIRST RATE BANK
OF MICHIGAN   No. 349

                        OCTOBER 9   19 81   10-00
                                                         000

PAY TO THE
ORDER OF   DR. RUTH MILLER $ 45.00

FORTY-FIVE and no/100 ～～～～～～～～ DOLLARS

MEMO CHECK UP   Richard Goldstein

1:0 2 1 3 ⬝⬝ 0 2 6 4 1:

Example 3.   This check is to Sun Power Company from Barbara Bolinski. It is for $25.34.

FIRST RATE BANK
OF MICHIGAN   No. 789

                        June 20   19 81   10-00
                                                      000
PAY TO THE
ORDER OF   Sun Power Company $ 25.34

Twenty-five and 34/100 ――――――― . DOLLARS

MEMO May utilities   Barbara Bolinski

1:0 2 1 3 ⬝⬝ 0 2 6 4 1:

Exercise 12

Write in the amounts of money on the checks.
Use numerals and words.

Eighty-nine dollars and fifty cents

FIRST RATE BANK
OF MICHIGAN

No. 129

December 9 19 _81_

10-00
000

PAY TO THE
ORDER OF _Veteran Heating Company_ $ _____

_____ DOLLARS

MEMO _furnace repair_

Shoshana Rose

⑃⑈021300381⑈: 319

$17.45

FIRST RATE BANK
OF MICHIGAN

No. 642

August 3 19 _81_

10-00
000

PAY TO THE
ORDER OF _Hamady's Market_ $ _____

_____ DOLLARS

MEMO _groceries_

Sarah E. Hamer

⑃⑈021300381⑈: 319

Two hundred eighty-five dollars

FIRST RATE BANK
OF MICHIGAN

No. 927

April 1 19 _81_

10-00
000

PAY TO THE
ORDER OF _Sam Burns_ $ _____

_____ DOLLARS

MEMO _June rent_ ———— _Jenny Santoro_

⑊:0213003 81: 318

$29.87

FIRST RATE BANK
OF MICHIGAN

No. 803

January 4 19 _81_

10-00
000

PAY TO THE
ORDER OF _Ace Hardware_ $ _____

_____ DOLLARS

MEMO _storm door parts_ ———— _Bob Jenkins_

⑊:0213003 81: 318

Answers for exercise 12

FIRST RATE BANK
OF MICHIGAN

No. 129

December 9   19 81   10-00 / 000

PAY TO THE
ORDER OF   Veteran Heating Company $ 89.50

Eighty-nine dollars and 50/100 ——————— DOLLARS

MEMO furnace repair   Shoshana Rose

⑈0213003811⑈ 319

FIRST RATE BANK
OF MICHIGAN

No. 642

August 3   19 81   10-00 / 000

PAY TO THE
ORDER OF   Hamady's Market $ 17.45

Seventeen dollars and 45/100 ——————— DOLLARS

MEMO groceries   Sarah E. Hamer

⑈0213003811⑈ 319

FIRST RATE BANK
OF MICHIGAN

No. 927

April 1   19 81   10-00 / 000

PAY TO THE
ORDER OF   Sam Burns $ 285.00

Two hundred eighty-five dollars and 00/100 ——— DOLLARS

MEMO June rent   Jenny Santoro

⑈0213003150⑈ 318

FIRST RATE BANK
OF MICHIGAN

No. 803

January 4   19 81   10-00 / 000

PAY TO THE
ORDER OF   Ace Hardware $ 29.87

Twenty-nine dollars and 87/100 ——————— DOLLARS

MEMO storm door parts   Bob Jenkins

⑈0213003150⑈ 318

Post-test

1. How many dots are in the box?

    ┌─────────────────────┐
    │ ● ● ● ● ● ● ● │   _____
    └─────────────────────┘

2. Write the numeral for this number: **two** _____

3. Write the word for this number: **7** _____

4. Write the numbers that are left out: **1,** _____**, 3, 4,** _____**,** _____**, 7, 8**

5. How many tens are in the number 86?   _____ **tens**

    How many ones are in the number 86?   _____ **ones**

6. Write the numeral for this number: **eleven**_____

7. Write the word for this number: **40** _____

8. Which number is biggest? Circle it.   **52   24   70**

9. Which number is biggest? Circle it.   **95   97   91**

10. Write the numeral for this number: **two hundred ninety**_____

11. How many hundreds are in 471?   _____ **hundreds**

12. Write the numeral for this word: **one thousand, four hundred sixteen**

    _____

13. What number comes next?   **99,998   99,999** _____

14. Write the numeral for this word: **Two hundred sixty-one dollars and three cents**

    _____

15. Write the numeral two ways: **Fifty cents** _____

    _____

Answers for post-test

1. 7
2. 2
3. seven
4. 2, 5, 6
5. 8 tens
   6 ones
6. 11
7. forty
8. 70
9. 97
10. 290
11. 4 hundreds
12. 1,416
13. 100,000
14. $261.03
15. $.50
    50¢

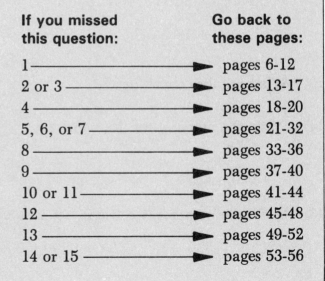

If you missed this question:	Go back to these pages:
1	pages 6-12
2 or 3	pages 13-17
4	pages 18-20
5, 6, or 7	pages 21-32
8	pages 33-36
9	pages 37-40
10 or 11	pages 41-44
12	pages 45-48
13	pages 49-52
14 or 15	pages 53-56